Discovering
WETLANDS

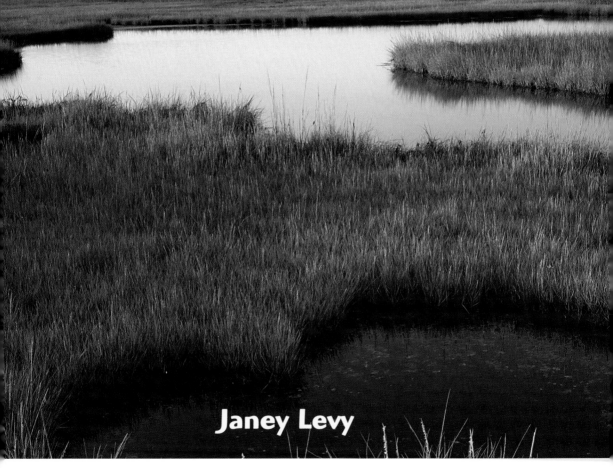

Janey Levy

PowerKiDS
press

New York

Published in 2008 by The Rosen Publishing Group, Inc.
29 East 21st Street, New York, NY 10010

First Edition

Editor: Geeta Sobha
Book Design: Julio Gil
Photo Researcher: Nicole Pristash

Photo Credits: Cover, p. 1 © Terry Donnelly/Getty Images; pp. 5, 6, 7, 8, 10, 12, 14, 16, 18, 20, 22, 24, 25, 27, 29 © www.shutterstock.com.

Library of Congress Cataloging-in-Publication Data

Levy, Janey.
  Discovering wetlands / Janey Levy. — 1st ed.
      p. cm. — (World habitats)
  Includes index.
  ISBN-13: 978-1-4042-3784-1 (lib. bdg.)
  ISBN-10: 1-4042-3784-4 (lib. bdg.)
  1. Wetlands—Juvenile literature. I. Title.
  QH87.3.L48 2008
  333.91'8—dc22
                                                    2006037809

Manufactured in Malaysia

Contents

What Is a Wetland?

A wetland is an area of land that is either wet all the time or only at certain times. Wetlands may be covered with water up to 6 feet (2 m) deep. They may also have little water on the surface but still be very wet because the groundwater, water stored inside the ground, is very close to the surface.

Wetlands occur in many kinds of places and in different shapes and sizes. However, all wetlands have three features. One feature is that they are covered with water or have water very near the surface at least

Ancient Wetlands and People

Plants and animals of wetlands have been an important part of people's diets for about 11,000 years. People began to plant and grow crops in wetlands about 9,000 years ago.

In November 2006, the Wings over Wetlands Project started a program to save wetlands between Africa and Eurasia for the benefit of migrating birds.

Female ducks will often return to breed in the same wetlands where they hatched.

part of the year. Another feature is that they have a special type of soil called hydric soil. This is soil formed under such wet conditions that it does not have much oxygen. The third feature is that wetland plants have adapted to the wet conditions with hydric soil. Many plants that grow elsewhere need more oxygen than is found in hydric soil.

The Climate of Wetlands

Wetlands are not limited to one kind of climate. They occur in every kind of climate on Earth. They can be found in places with Arctic, temperate, and tropical climates.

Wetlands in Arctic climates may have temperatures as low as -60° F (-51° C)! Wetlands in temperate climates experience warm summers and cold winters. Wetlands in tropical climates may have temperatures as high as 122° F (50° C)!

Mangrove trees have roots that grow above the water. These trees grow in places along coasts where there is salt water.

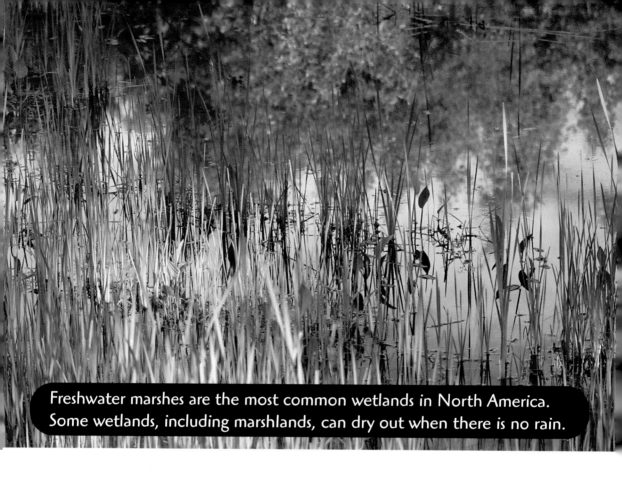

Freshwater marshes are the most common wetlands in North America. Some wetlands, including marshlands, can dry out when there is no rain.

Wetlands receive varying amounts of rain. Some wetlands receive as little as 6 inches (15 cm) of rain each year. Others receive as much as 200 inches (508 cm)!

Why do wetlands have so many different climates? It is because they occur in so many different regions of Earth. Let's take a look at where wetlands are found.

Where in the World Are Wetlands?

Wetlands cover about 6 percent of Earth's land surface. They extend from the Arctic regions of the Far North to the tropical regions around the equator and then south to the temperate regions of southern South America and southern Australia. Every continent except Antarctica has wetlands. Africa has more wetlands than any other continent.

Wetlands are found along the coast of oceans and lakes and along the edges of ponds, rivers, and streams. They are also found far away from bodies of water, in low-lying areas where rain collects or groundwater comes to the surface.

Every state in the United States has some kind of wetlands. Wetlands cover about 250 million acres (101 million ha) of the country. Alaska has more than half the wetlands in the United States.

Kinds of Wetlands

There are three main kinds of wetlands: marshes, swamps, and peatlands. Each kind has several varieties.

Marshes constitute about 90 percent of all wetlands. Two types exist, freshwater and saltwater. Plants such as grasses, reeds, sedges, and rice grow in marshes.

Freshwater marshes, usually found in temperate climates, commonly appear along the edges of lakes, rivers, and streams. Other freshwater marshes include seasonal types, such as wet meadows, prairie potholes, and vernal pools. Wet meadows are grasslands with very wet soil. Prairie potholes are small marshes in low-lying prairie regions. Vernal pools are shallow areas that fill with rainwater in spring and dry up in summer.

Black spruce trees, shown here, grow in wetlands of Alaska.

Saltwater marshes occur in coastal areas. Only grasses that have adapted to seawater's high salt content grow here.

Swamps are similar to marshes, but they have mostly trees and shrubs. Both freshwater and saltwater swamps exist. Freshwater swamps appear along rivers and streams. Saltwater swamps occur in coastal areas.

Pocosins

Although most swamps occur in low-lying areas, some do not. These swamps are called pocosins. The name comes from a Native American term that means "swamp on a hill."

Peatlands are freshwater wetlands where peat has formed. Two kinds exist, bogs and fens.

Bogs constitute about 90 percent of peatlands and mostly occur in temperate climates. They have acidic soil and are covered by moss. Tropical bogs

In unhealthy water conditions, algae can grow in great quantities, taking over wetlands, such as the swamp shown here.

Plants in wetlands can provide food and shelter for many animals.

are called tree bogs because the peat forms from rotting trees rather than moss.

Fens are similar to bogs. However, fens do not have acidic soil, and they have grasses, sedges, and reeds instead of moss.

Wetland Plants

Scientists often divide wetland plants into four groups. Submergents are plants that grow completely underwater. Floating plants have leaves that float on the water's surface. Some floating plants are rooted in the soil below the water, but others float freely. Emergents are plants with leaves and stems sticking up above the water. Woody plants are trees and shrubs. In addition to these groups, mosses are also common in wetlands.

Dinosaur Food?

One common freshwater marsh emergent is often called river pumpkin because its leaves resemble pumpkin leaves. It has been around for 95 million years. Plant-eating dinosaurs may have dined on this plant!

Freshwater marshes have many emergent plants, such as grasses, forbs, sedges, rushes, and reeds. They also have floating plants, such as duckweed and water lilies, and submergents, such as coontail and water milfoil. Saltwater marshes

have emergent grasses, such as cordgrass and salt-meadow grass.

Freshwater swamps have woody plants. Trees include maples, birches, cypresses, cedars, and spruces. Shrubs include willows and dogwood. Freshwater swamps also have emergents, such as grasses, forbs, and sedges.

The best-known saltwater swamps are mangrove swamps. Mangrove trees have unusual roots. They are visible because they come out of the trees above the water. This results from the lack of air in the water and soil.

Bogs have mosses and emergents, such as grasses and sedges. They may also have woody plants, such as evergreen trees and shrubs. Unusual bog plants include sundews and pitcher plants, which both eat insects.

Fens have emergents, such as sedges and rushes. They may also have woody shrubs.

Water lilies are plants with roots in the soil at the bottom of the water and flowers and leaves drifting at the water's surface.

Frogs are animals that need wetlands to live. They lay their eggs in water, and the tadpoles that hatch live in the water.

Wetland Animals

Wetlands are important to wild animals in ways you might not think of at first. Of course, many animals live in wetlands. In addition, other animals live near wetlands and go there to find food and water. These include minks, moose, falcons, otters, bears, raccoons, deer, reindeer, wolves, kangaroos, rats, and some fish. Migrating birds, including ducks, geese, and swans, also use wetlands. Some stop there to rest and feed during their migration. Others use wetlands for nesting and breeding. Animals such as frogs, toads, salamanders, and some insects spend the first stage of their lives in wetlands.

A Spider Trick

Water spiders living in wetlands have a special trick to help them live through winter. They create an air bubble deep in the water and live inside it until spring, protected from the cold.

Freshwater marsh animals include fish, alligators, crocodiles, eagles, beavers, bobcats, egrets, cranes, worms, mosquitoes and other insects, spiders, snails, frogs, turtles, jaguars, and monkeys. All these animals are not found in the same marshes.

Saltwater marsh animals include fish, snakes, alligators, crocodiles, frogs and other amphibians, insects including beetles and flies, birds, mice, and seals. Different animals live in different marshes.

Animals found in various freshwater swamps include alligators, crocodiles, turtles, fish, beavers, bobcats, eagles, egrets, cranes, worms, frogs, mosquitoes and other insects, spiders, snails, and crayfish. Animals that live in saltwater swamps include alligators, crocodiles, fish, oysters, crabs, worms, pelicans, wading birds, bats, and insects. Bog and fen animals include beetles, butterflies, mosquitoes, geese, owls, ducks, hawks, frogs, and salamanders.

Alligators live in wetlands, such as swamps and marshes. They feed mainly at night.

Monarch butterflies can be found in open areas, such as marshes and meadows. They are poisonous and can cause sickness in animals that eat them.

Florida's Everglades

Florida's Everglades are the most famous wetlands in the United States. They cover about 5,500 square miles (14,245 sq km) in southern Florida. They include both freshwater and saltwater marshes and swamps.

The Kissimmee River and Lake Okeechobee provide water for the freshwater marshes and swamps. Important plants include sawgrass and cypress trees. There are also floating plants, such as water lilies.

The Vanishing Everglades

Ever since the first colonists arrived, people have been turning the Everglades into dry land for crops and buildings. The Everglades once covered about 11,000 square miles (28,490 sq km)—twice the area they cover today!

Saltwater marshes and swamps occur along the coasts of the Atlantic Ocean and the Gulf of Mexico. Important plants include sea grass and mangrove trees.

The reddish egret hunts for fish in the Everglades' waters. It lifts its wings over the water to block glare so that it can see fish easier.

The Everglades' animals include storks, egrets, raccoons, skunks, opossums, bobcats, deer, snakes, alligators, and rare Florida panthers. Fish, manatees, and dolphins live in the coastal waters.

The Importance of Wetlands

People used to think wetlands had no value, so they removed the water to create dry land for planting crops or building towns. However, people have slowly come to realize that wetlands are important for many reasons.

As you have learned from reading this book, many kinds of plants and animals live in wetlands or depend on them for food, water, and breeding. Without wetlands, these plants and animals would cease to exist.

Turtles use wetland pools to cool their bodies during hot summer days.

Wetlands help prevent flooding. They act like sponges and take in water from heavy rains or melting snow. Then they slowly let out the water into streams, rivers, lakes, and the ground. In a similar way, coastal wetlands provide protection from storms such as hurricanes.

Wetlands also help clean our drinking water. Water that comes into wetlands is often polluted and dirty. Wetlands remove the dirt and polluted matter from the water.

Saving Water

Just 1 acre of wetlands can hold about 1.5 million gallons (5.7 million l) of water and prevent floods from happening.

Wetlands store carbon in plants and soil instead of putting it into the air as carbon dioxide. That helps prevent problems such as global warming. These are just some of the ways wetlands help make our world a better place.

Many wetlands form around lakes, which are important sources of freshwater that can be used for drinking.

Protecting Wetlands

Many people are now working to prevent further loss of wetlands. Federal, state, and local governments are passing laws to protect wetlands. Many people are working to educate the public about wetlands' importance. However, much work remains to be done. Here are some things you can do to help.

- Find out about wetlands near your home and help educate others about them.
- Learn about local projects to renew lost wetlands and help with those.
- Buy duck stamps from the post office. The money is used to care for wetlands.
- Plan a program about wetlands at your school.

Wetlands are important. We must all work together to protect them.

Protecting wetlands will also help keep the wildlife living in those areas safe.

Wetland Facts and Figures

- Retreating glaciers formed many wetlands about 11,000 years ago.

- Wetlands have more kinds of plants and animals than almost any other type of region.

- Peatland covers about 1.5 million square miles (3.9 million sq km) worldwide.

- Mangrove trees cover about 34 million acres (13.8 million ha) worldwide.

- A saltwater marsh produces 5 to 10 times as much oxygen as an equal area of wheat.

- In 1 acre (.4 ha) of wetland, there can be 1.5 million gallons (5.7 million l) of floodwater stored.

- Seventy-five percent of waterfowl breed only in wetlands.

- More than one-third of the animals in the United States that are in danger of vanishing live only in wetlands.

- About half the world's wetlands have vanished since 1900.

- The United States loses more than 100,000 acres (40,500 ha) of wetlands annually.

Glossary

carbon dioxide (KAR-bin dy-OK-syd) A gas produced by rotting plants. Too much of it in the air can raise Earth's temperature.

equator (ih-KWAY-tur) The imaginary line around Earth that separates it into two parts, northern and southern.

forbs (FORBZ) Small plants with broad leaves.

hurricanes (HUR-ih-kaynz) Storms with strong winds and heavy rain.

manatees (MA-nuh-teez) Large plant-eating ocean animals that live in coastal waters. Manatees are related to elephants.

migrating (MY-grayt-ing) Moving from one place to another.

peat (PEET) Partly rotted plant matter found in some wetlands. Peat has partly turned into carbon.

peatlands (PEET-landz) The type of wetlands where peat is found. Bogs and fens are peatlands.

rushes (RUSH-ez) Grasslike plants that grow near water.

sedges (SEJ-ez) Grasslike marsh plants.

temperate (TEM-puh-rut) Not too hot or too cold.

tropical (TRAH-puh-kul) Having to do with the warm parts of Earth that are near the equator.

waterfowl (WAH-ter-fowl) Ducks, geese, swans, and similar waterbirds.

Index

Web Sites

Due to the changing nature of Internet links, PowerKids Press has developed an online list of Web sites related to the subject of this book. This site is updated regularly. Please use this link to access the list: www.powerkidslinks.com/whab/wetland/